# Auschwitz And The Holocaust

*Discover The Truth Of What Really Happened In The Nazi Death Camps: The Chilling Stories Of Auschwitz And The Holocaust*

V. Jaydon

inattention or otherwise, by any usage or abuse of any policies, processes, or directions contained within is the solitary and utter responsibility of the recipient reader. Under no circumstances will any legal responsibility or blame be held against the publisher for any reparation, damages, or monetary loss due to the information herein, either directly or indirectly.

V. Jaydon

# **Table of Contents**

# Want more books?

Would you love books delivered straight to your inbox every week?

Free?

How about non-fiction books on all kinds of subjects?

We send out e-books to our loyal subscribers every week to download and enjoy!

All you have to do is join! It's so easy!

Just visit the link at the end of this book to sign up and then wait for your books to arrive!

# Introduction

Many historians have explained the holocaust and the tragedy of the Second World War. How did one evil man convince millions of good people to want to destroy their neighbors' homes, family, traditions, religion and life? Was it a mass delusion? Was it just about the money?

Some believe the holocaust didn't even happen. Some believe the wars of today are simulated. Many people in the 30's and 40's didn't believe the phone calls, greeting cards and letters they received with warning signs from the feared death camps all over Europe.....

Still, millions of innocent people perished in front of everyone's eyes. Let's take a look at Auschwitz and the Holocaust.

Thanks again for purchasing this book, I hope you enjoy it!

# Chapter 1: The Nazis And How They Got Their Power

World War I left Germany devastated. Politically, economically and socially. The atmosphere was gloomy and charged. The victorious Great Britain, United States and France punished Germany severely.

After the treaty of Versailles, German pride was not the only one to suffer. Germany was forced to give territory to its neighbors, pay huge reparations, admit and accept the responsibility for the war and limit their military to only 100,000 troops.

The responsible political and military elite claimed they had been stabbed in the back by their opponents: the left-wing parties, Jews and communists. Imperial Germany was replaced with the Weimar Republic, but this federal republic couldn't handle the depressed economy either.

At the time, the Nazi Party was known as German Workers' Party, a small ideological body gathering demobilized soldiers. In 1919, Hitler joined the party with his views of a racially pure Germany, national pride, commitment to the Volk and militarism. His captivating speeches made him leader of the party after only two years. He changed the name of the party to National

Socialist German Workers' Party, NSDAP or Nazi Party.

In 1923, his attempt to take over the government ended in failure. The courtroom didn't stay indifferent to his emotional speeches, so he was released from jail after serving only one year. While in jail, he wrote the book ***Mein Kampf (My Struggle),*** where he laid down his political (racist, anti-Bolshevistic and nationalistic) ideology and revolutionary plans for the future of Germany.

When he got out of jail, he tried to resurrect his party. They couldn't successfully infiltrate into the big cities, so his party gained only 2.6% of the votes in the 1928 elections. From only 3000 unemployed soldiers in 1919, to 27, 000 members in 1925, the party counted 108,000 like-minded people in 1929.

The great depression wrought more than 6 million unemployed people in Germany. The new economic downturn worked to Hitler's advantage because he could practice his psychological games, easily convincing people that their poor economic situation was a result of up-and-coming Jewish (and other minorities) agricultural properties, businesses and department stores.

The job of gaining support in Berlin, as well as building an overpowering propaganda was given to Goebbels, where he excelled. His propaganda proved to be working mainly on young lower middle class men, university students and veterans' organizations.

The president and army hero, Paul von Hindenburg formed a new government, where each chancellor and minister would be ruled by an emergency decree. This brought the beginning of the fall of the Weimar democracy. The newly appointed chancellor Heinrich Bruning could not unify the government, so in 1930, Germany scheduled new elections.

Over 18% votes made the Nazi party the second largest political party in the Weimar Republic. Hindenburg had to select a new chancellor. He disliked Hitler, and Hitler knew this, so he proposed (pressured) a coalition with the Center Party and the Social Democrat Party.

Each of them would have to work to keep one third of the seats of the parliament, and Hitler was supposed to be made chancellor. Both parties were afraid to stand against Hitler and his organized squads, so they agreed to the deal.

In 1933, Hindenburg was pressured to make Hitler chancellor; Hitler became the head of the government. A year later, Hindenburg died, and Hitler joined the offices of the Chancellor and President, and became the Fuhrer of Germany.

## The Nazis and the Communists

Following the example of Mussolini's Blackshirts, Hitler formed the Brownshirts, or SA (Sturmabteilung or Storm Troopers). The SS (Schutzstaffelor Protection Squad) were formed as an elite unit for personal protection of Hitler, but during the war, they would be the main instrument of terror that occurred all over Europe.

By the end of 1934, the SA and SS controlled the security system and police in Germany, thanks to many organized, extreme infiltration techniques. They were used for street brawling, increasing fright and spreading propaganda. They were used to break up meetings of the communist party and beat up opponents in the middle of the street.

Between 1931 and 1933, the violence between the Nazi SA and the communist Rotfront spiralled out of control, counting 47 victims on the SA side and 80 on the Rotfront side. After the presidential elections in 1932, the government banned the SA and SS, action encouraged after a trial of SA men who assaulted Jews in Berlin.

The chancellor of the time, Papen, revoked the ban, which led Rotfront to turn to more violence instead of political debate. The attacks multiplied and reached a boiling point when the SA leader was killed. This led the president of the parliament to propose amendments to the Reichstrafgesetzbuch statute, on the act of political violence, where the penalty was increased to lifetime prison, 20 years of hard labor and death.

5 Nazis who were sentenced under the new laws were released after 4 months imprisonment, when the Nazi party won the elections, in 1933. Later, Hitler used these laws to his advantage, to imprison anyone who opposed his views.

The communist party had quantifiable influence even after the appointment of Adolf Hitler as chancellor. He became chancellor in January, but was not sure that his party would win the national elections in March the same year. So in February the Reichstag building (the parliament building) was set on fire.

Hitler and Goebbels had dinner together, when Dr. Hansfstaengl called Goebbels and told him that the parliament building was on fire. When Hitler found out, he accused the communists and ordered every one of them to be shot where they were found and their deputies hanged the same night.

Over 4000 people were arrested and a young Dutch communist named Marius van der Lubbe took the blame.

After the interrogation, the Prussian political police found his confession too fanciful to be true, but Lubbe was sentenced anyway.

It was widely believed that the fire was ordered by Goebbels and executed by SA members. He knew that the party could not win the elections, so he had to do something to boost their odds. Members of the SS were then ordered to kill the members of the SA who burnt down the building, so there would be no witnesses. This theory was suggested by Martin Sommerfeldt, a government employee and backed up by Rudolf Diels, a Gestapo chief.

**Life During Nazi's Reign**

A couple of months after the Reichstag Fire, on the 5th of March, the Nazi Party won 44% of the votes and 288 seats in the parliament. Later the same month, the Enabling Act was passed in the parliament and the Reichsrat, and signed by the president Hindenburg. This act allowed the chancellor Hitler to make his own laws without any involvement or agreement of the parliament.

With the Reichstag Fire Decree, Germany under dictatorship was born. This decree annulled many civil liberties. The SA squad had the right and privilege to go after and intimidate communists, non-Nazi deputies and anyone who didn't agree to their ideology. The communist party was banned. Germany was divided into 42 Gaus with local governments, controlled by 42 Gauleiters.

The Gestapo secret police was formed and they were allowed to kill and imprison anyone without trial or interrogation. The leaders of all trade unions were arrested and the unions abolished. Only the German Labor Front was in function of the workers, where it was made sure that only Nazis were employed. All other political parties were banned and membership in the Nazi party was mandatory. In the people's court, the judges (Nazi members) no longer swore to God, they swore an oath of loyalty to the Nazi party.

All these changes happened within a year of Hitler's appointment as chancellor. The Nazi regime ruined the democracy, the country became a police state, with only one separate body – the army. By the middle of the 1934, Hitler realized that he couldn't control the SS squad.

He went after the SS and their leader Ernest Rohm, because their growing power was a serious threat to his regime. Rohm wanted the Stormtroopers to be the core of the states' military defense, the army wanted the paramilitary squad disarmed, so Hitler took advantage of this situation to neutralize both bodies.

The army made an agreement to demonstrate loyalty to the Nazi party only if Hitler disarmed the SA. So, he organized the Night of the Long Knives or Operation Hummingbird, which was a purge that took place between June 30 and July 2. The SS reported killings of over 85 political enemies of Hitler and the new regime, but the numbers may have been in the hundreds.

Thousands were arrested, which were the first captives in the concentration camps near Berlin. Leading political figures were murdered, including Gregor Strasser of the left wing of the Nazi party, Kurt von Schleicher (former chancellor) and Gustav Ritter von Kahr, the suppressor of his putsch 10 years ago. Almost all leaders of the SS squad were killed too, which secured Hitler with a dictatorship position without opponents, critics or independence from the Nazi party.

If you were on the side of the winning Nazi party however, your life during this time would not be at all bad. Hitler gained people's trust by convincing them they were the only race worth living. He had a stance from where all non-Aryan people should not have a say in Germany, only the master race should live and prosper.

Hitler wanted to get rid of the people with physical and mental disabilities, because they drained the resources of his Aryan master race. If you were a Nazi, you could get a good job, attend ceremonies, rallies and work programs. Family life was valued and marriage highly appreciated. Married couples got 1000 marks from the government and 250 marks for each child. Those mothers who had over 8 children were given golden medals.

The third Reich was antifeminist, male dominated society, where the role of the woman was a role of a child bearer. All women who had careers had to give up their jobs to a man. Young boys were particularly cherished by the Reich. Young girls had to focus on the 3 C's – church, children, cooking. All kids were told to report to the Gestapo if their parents criticized Hitler or his party.

All foreign books and records were destroyed and only German culture was allowed, Wagner and Beethoven, German approved authors and Nazi actors. If you played foreign music or movie or owned a book not by a pre-approved German author, you could've been very easily sentenced to death. Interestingly, most of the people approved of the regime. After one world war, a great depression, civil wars and blood on the streets, the German nation saw the Nazis as saviours and protectors.

# Chapter 2: Holocaust: The Final Solution to the Jewish Question

The holocaust was an assembly of events that happened exclusively around Europe, during the 20th century.

It started slowly in the 30's right after Hitler's appointment as chancellor, and progressed until the end of the Second World War. The events accumulated, one after another, until the early 40's, when the Jewish people were treated like animals. There were 11 million Jewish people living in Europe in 1941.

When the war was over, the Nazis had documentation for the killings of 6 million of them, one and a half of which were children. Whole families were captured together, grandparents, parents and children. The Nazis were rampant towards many societal groups, not just the Jewish people. Hitler imprisoned homosexuals, opponents of all types, Romani people, people with disabilities and people who hid someone they wanted imprisoned.

Before his generals thought of organizing the death camps, they were killed with lethal injections, sterilized or imprisoned and used for hard human labor.

It was soon very clear that Hitler's ideals for Germany

included many other countries. In 1938 he invaded Austria, and parts of Czechoslovakia. A year later he controlled all Czechoslovakia and invaded Poland, which started the Second World War.

Later he occupied Belgium, Netherlands, Luxembourg, Denmark, Norway, France, Yugoslavia and Greece. Suddenly in the mind of the dictator, the Jewish people were to blame for everything that was wrong in Europe, not just Germany.

# German's Racial Superiority

In his book Mein Kampf, Hitler outlined his racial principles. When he became the head of government he enforced a new law to Prevent Hereditarily Diseased Offspring. Because he and his party believed every Jew was the source of all evil, they tried to administer the removal of the "undesirables".

This law did not affect racial groups exclusively; all mentally and physically impaired people were not allowed to reproduce also. They sterilized or killed many deaf or blind people, people who suffered from feeble-mindedness, manic-depressive disorder, epilepsy, schizophrenia, Huntington's chorea, severe physical deformities and chronic alcoholism.

In the next 18 months, the law allowed the Nazi state to sterilize over 400,000 people, who didn't fit Hitler's vision of the "master race"

The Nazi propaganda of German superiority was inflicted through television, movies, and radio and in schools. Children were checked and measured for certain qualities that defined the eugenic ideal or Aryan race. Their noses' length had to fit a certain scale, so did their skulls. They had to be blonde, blue eyed and tall. Those who fit the description were called Übermensch, which means superman. All others were considered Untermensch, or sub-humans.

A racial hierarchy divided people into important and unimportant groups. At the bottom of the pyramid were dark skinned people, indigenous to Africa and Australia. They were thought to be mentally and physically inferior to the Aryan race.

People from southern Europe, with their dark hair and eyes, and olive skin were in the middle of the pyramid. They were considered impure because their genes were mixed with the Untermensch. Only Germans, Swedes, Norwegians, Icelanders, Danes, English and Dutch were at the top of the pyramid, and they made the superior race.

Blue eyed and blond men, taller than 6ft were especially honored by Hitler. They were immediately given officer titles in the SS unit and a golden medal. These people were called Hünenmensch (literally, megalithic people) and were thought to be direct offspring of the ancient warriors of the German tribes from where the Aryan race descended. If however, it was established that your unusual height was just a result of a defective pituitary gland, your only reward would've been sterilization.

The law to Prevent Hereditarily Diseased Offspring safely

and completely carried out the elimination of the unfit, but Hitler wanted to make sure the Aryan race was multiplying fast. He created the Lebensborn program, which had racially pure German SS members impregnate Aryan women in specially designed facilities for that purpose.

When the war ended, there were 42,000 Aryan babies born under the program. The SS soldiers were allowed to kidnap Aryan children from the countries the Nazis invaded. From Poland alone, they captured over 200,000 children.

## What is Anti-Semitism?

The term anti-Semitism was first used in 1897, but the anti-Jewish feelings had provoked violence and hostility for more than 2000 years. It was called the Longest Hatred, because Jews were accused for many societal, economic and political upheavals throughout history.

It all started with the crucifixion of Christ. Even though Jesus was Jewish, just like his disciples, and even if their prayers were in Hebrew and the oldest bible was written in Hebrew, the world still believed that the Jews were responsible for the deicide.

Just after the crucifixion, Jews were exiled from Israel.

They scattered throughout Europe, where by the 5th century, Christianity was the dominant religion. The early Roman Church depicted Jews as evil, followers of the devil and accused them for the killing of the messiah.

It was believed they used Christian children for rituals, where they drained their blood as a sacrifice. They were not allowed to hold public positions, offices and land. Most professions were outlawed for the Jews and they had to engage in money landing businesses, commerce and trading.

Martin Luther reformed the Catholic Church and thought he could convert the Jews. When he saw they adhered to their own religion, he turned to violence instead of tolerance. He called them condemned, ordered their synagogues to be destroyed and buried, their houses demolished and prayer books burnt.

Their lingering condemnation never seemed to stop. Not even during the 18th century, when philosophers emphasized on reason and the influence if the church was diminished. In some circles, it was whispered that they could become equal members of the society only if they abandon their traditions and religion. Other thinkers criticized their customs as a source of unreasonable religious faith.

## What Is The Final Solution?

Prejudice and hatred became a part of every Jewish life, but their discrimination has never reached a brutal level like during the Third Reich. At first the Nazi party wanted to make sure they couldn't assimilate in the society meant only for the master race, but later, their ideals concentrated on the most inhumane and systematic methods of genocide history has ever known. This was a program known as the Final Solution to the Jewish Question.

The program's plan was to exterminate every living Jew in Europe. When the Nazi party gained power in 1933, their main focus was to take over the businesses from the Jews, their money and properties. When this stage of the plan was implemented, the SS units started to use terror and intimidation to force them to migrate.

Jews were not allowed to live in the cities, go to school or have public jobs. Everyone who had at least two Jewish grandparents was considered a Jew and was stripped of their German citizenship. They were systematically transferred to ghettos, from where later; their allocation into camps was easier.

The fate of the Jews (the ones who survived the regime)

was finally determined with the Wannsee Conference in 1942. The first option was to clean room on German ground by transferring Jews on Madagascar. This idea was voted as impractical.

Later it was suggested they be relocated in Siberia as slaves or murdered. It was estimated that around 8 million Jews already lived in Russia and Ukraine, so the final plan was created – to kill all Jewish people in the Soviets and relocate everyone else into concentration camps.

The SS had a special mobile unit designed for locating and murdering Jews on the spot. Reinhard Heydrich chief of the SS, invited representatives from the justice ministry, ministry of interior affairs, secretaries from the foreign office and members of the SS at the convention, to help determine the best plan for extermination.

They decided to transfer European Jews in concentration camps and mobile units were sent to execute the Jews living in the Soviet Union. The reports of Jewish killings from the Soviet Union after the war varied, where one source stated there were only a few thousand killed, others said several million.

By the time the conference ended, thousands of Jews were killed all over Europe. After the slaughter in the Soviet

Union, Himmler, a leading member of the Nazi party, military commander and one of the people directly responsible for the holocaust, decided it would be better for all Jews to be imprisoned in concentration camps. That way, deaths would've been faster and less personal for the shooters, who wanted to avoid emotional anguish.

# Chapter 3: The Main Camp and the Monowitz

Auschwitz I was the first extermination camp (Main Camp) used by the Third Reich. Last used by the Polish army, the camp consisted of 16 one-story brick barracks, suitable to host the first prisoners of the Reich. During the war, the camp was a working place for nearly 7000 SS soldiers and officers.

The first prisoners to arrive were Polish political opponents of the regime, members of the intelligentsia and Soviet resistance fighters. In the course of the war, the camp housed 150,000 Poles, 15,000 Soviet prisoners, 23,000 Romani (and Sinti), 400 Jehovah's Witnesses, other people from diverse nationality and homosexuals. 1 in 6 Jews who died in the holocaust, died in Auschwitz I.

The words "Arbeit macht frei" (Work Will Make You Free) greeted the prisoners, preparing them for the hard labor they were about to carry out and the hope that work would free them, which was rarely the case.

The main camp later became the administrative center of the entire extermination complex. An additional 28, two-story buildings were added by the end of 1944. Run by Rudolf Hess, who like many other SS officers, lived within the camp, together with his wife and children.

In one private letter, his wife wrote to her relatives that they lived in a beautiful house, overlooking a lake and they were having a lot of fun. Their house was located 20m away from a gas chamber and the lake she mentioned, was the lake that gathered the remains of the Jewish people burnt in a crematorium not so far away. The first victims of the Reich were executed in the main camp, but gassing slowed down once the second camp was built.

Auschwitz III (Monowitz) was an industrial complex built by prisoners after the SS signed a contract with the German IG Farben Company, for liquid fuel and synthetic rubber. The executives saw a convenient opportunity to take advantage of the cheap human labor, so they built their complex near the main concentration camp.

The company paid 4 marks per hour for skilled employees, 3 marks per day for unskilled personnel and 1 ½ marks for children. 10,000 prisoners died on this ground, some from exhaustion, others from hunger and countless victims collapsed under the brutal hands of the SS soldiers.

Life expectancy was between 3 and 4 months. Those slaves who completely lost their strength and health while working in the Monowitz camp were taken in the nearby Auschwitz Birkenau and killed in gas chambers. Another 25,000 deaths happened following this particular directive, according to the IG Farben Company record books.

These prisoners records were signed "nach Birkenau" (to Birkenau), which was a euphemism for sending the prisoner to a gas chamber. Primo Levi and Elie Wiesel were the two survivors who worked in this camp, both wrote extensively about life during the regime.

# Chapter 4: The Horrors of Auschwitz II

After the main camp became overcrowded, Auschwitz II was built. Historians estimated execution of prisoners in this camp to be between the numbers of 2 and 4 million.

At the beginning of 1941, this camp retained less than 20,000 prisoners, most of them Jews. After Himmler's visit the same year, the camp was enlarged to fit at least 100,000 prisoners. Its location was most suitable because the railroad from the Jewish quart in Krakow extended to the entrance of Auschwitz Birkenau.

Sections of the camp were established to keep the women and men separated, as well as other nationalities from the Jews. The camp had two gas chambers which formed brick cottages. By 1943, the Nazi generals were not content with the gassing capacity of the gas chambers, so the crematorium II was built.

What was formerly used as a mortuary, now was turned into a little death factory. With the renovation, a gas-tight door and a ventilation system was added, a construction that made the extermination faster and easier. Using the same design, crematoria III, IV and V were built later that year.

# Arrival to the Death Camps

There was no discussion about what would happen to Jews after the Final Solution was decided. People all over Europe were loaded into cattle trucks and wagons and transported to Auschwitz. The wagons were packed full, there was no room to sit inside. The prisoners only had a bucket of water and an empty bucket to serve them as a toilet.

They didn't know where they would be taken when they were dragged out of the ghettos, so most of them had only their clothes on their back. The journey to the death camps sometimes lasted for days. People were hungry, thirsty and some of them got sick. Many didn't even make it to Auschwitz because they died of suffocation, hunger or as a result of the cold weather.

They were unloaded at the gates of Auschwitz II, where SS officers and doctors decided their fate. Dr. Mengele was always at the scene, as he was in charge of choosing the victims for his medical experiments. The SS officers did their selection. All people who were sick, too old or unable to work were sent straight to the gas chambers.

The teenage girls and boys were left alive, because they were considered most fit to work. Men and women were separated, children stayed with their mothers. Pregnant women were taken by the doctors for medical experiments. Those lucky enough to survive the selection, were stripped naked and shaved. All their hair had to be removed. The barbers, usually men, used dull objects and worked fast, so most of the prisoners ended up injured.

Jewish women were humiliated during this process, when they had to stand naked in front of several SS soldiers and officers, while being made fun of. They were given striped uniforms with numbers, and the same numbers were tattooed on their left forearm.

The guards had to tell them apart, so every uniform had a sewed or painted triangle. A red one meant political prisoner, green one- professional criminal, black one- asocial, purple- catholic, pink- homosexual, violet- Jehovah's witness, and a yellow star meant the prisoner was Jewish.

This triangular piece of cloth was called the Winkel and the guards made use of it to distinguish between not only the prisoners' race or religion, but also their nationality. Political prisoners wore a red colored triangular cloth. On the cloth was an alphabet that was generally stitched in – this alphabet was representative of the country they had been deported from and the nationality they belonged to.

And if there was a prisoner who belonged to more than a

single category, they were forced to wear all the colors they were assigned to. For instance, a gay Jewish man would have to wear both the pink Winkel as well as the yellow star. It would be sewn into his shirt and he would be given absolutely no choice in the matter.

As if that wasn't enough, the Nazis went on to allot each prisoner a number to identify them with as well. Of course, allotting numbers to prisoners is quite a common practice, even in today's world, but the Nazi didn't just give them numbers or have it sewn into their clothes -- they had it tattooed on their very skins, as though the men and women literally were allowed to have no identity of their own, except for the number that they were allotted and the Winkel they wore.

All their personal possessions were taken away, because they were considered just numbers once they stepped foot in the camp. Trains were arriving several times a day in Auschwitz II, where 80% of the prisoners were murdered the same hour.

Those who were left alive for labor were put in quarantine. There, they had the worst time because some of them, for the first time were finding out what was going on. There, they got to meet their tormenters, the rules and what happened if they didn't obey. They realized that they may never see their relatives again.

The day for the prisoners began at 3 or 4 a clock in the morning with a Roll Call. This meant they had to wake up, get out in front of their barracks, stand in rows and wait for the SS officers to count them. Such early hours were picked intentionally, to make the prisoners wait a long time for the officers to arrive.

They sometimes stayed still for hours, regardless of the weather. They were ordered not to move or talk, otherwise, they would end up being shot. Those who weren't exhausted from working long hours were either too sick or too hungry. Occasionally, one of the prisoners would collapse onto their neighbor, and because they were too weak to hold their collapsed inmate, all of them would fall down like dominos.

This was very amusing for the officers, who made a habit of pushing one to make them all fall down. If one of the prisoners didn't stand still during the Roll Call, they were forced to run until they fainted. When the officers arrived they would count the prisoners.

The number had to be the same as the previous day. If there was one prisoner too many, the weakest one was taken to a gas chamber. If they killed too many the previous day, the numbers were evened up with the new arrivals. That was why many murders between the prisoners occurred; they were pushed to fight for their own lives.

Not only were they expected to stand for hours together, they were forced to stand even with the dead. Roll Call occasionally also included the dead bodies of the prisoners who were too weak or tired to make it in the bitter cold of the morning and ended up dying while awaiting the officers to come.

Lined up in rows of five, if a single prisoner dropped, no one stopped to even give them a second look – survivors remember that they had no choice but to watch as their fellow inmates were propped up, their bodies already rotting in the elements but given no respect by the Nazis.

They didn't stop there. At Roll Call, the guards took explicit pleasure in making things horrid for the inmates and treated them like toys to be played with. They would often find excuses – not real reasons, but rather flimsy, easy jokes – to whip, hurt or torture the prisoners at their whims and fancies.

Many an Auschwitz survivor recalled being beaten up for having a missing button on their already tattered clothes or being whipped mercilessly because they had not cleaned out a food bowl properly. Much of the punishment meted out was meant as a signal for the rest of the prisoners to toe the line; the Nazis enjoyed the brutality and making an example out of their victims and their torture reflected that ideal quite clearly.

After the Roll Call was finally completed, the prisoners were sent to their workstations. Between Roll Calls and work hours, the prisoners were forced to learn German songs, take off their caps at the sight of an officer and greet them with the Nazi or Hitler salute. The songs were sung on their way to work.

The clothes they were given were flimsy at best and were hardly enough to guard them against the bitter cold that they were often exposed to. Underwear was a rare luxury that was almost never afforded to them, as were protection for their feet.

More often than not, they had to go bare foot amongst the harsh elements; socks and proper footwear were almost never given to them. Even if they did receive footwear, it was usually in the form of ugly, wooden shoes that were of poor quality – they hardly fit and were generally more trouble than they were worth.

## Their Work and Routine in the Camp

There were many German factories near the camps, where the prisoners were used as cheap labor. There were a variety of jobs, from heavy manual labor like construction and coal mining, to administration tasks and farming. Working sites were several kilometers away, which the workers had to walk to every day, poorly dressed and fed.

Not all prisoners worked away from the camp, there were chores inside the camp as well. Prisoners were responsible for order in the barracks. They were called kapos. The workers who prepared the prisoners for gassing were called sonderkommandos. They further transferred dead bodies into the crematoria.

Usually, the strongest people were chosen for this job. There was another sub-unit, called Kanada Kommando. These workers had to go over the possessions of the prisoners who just arrived. Jewelry and other valuables were taken away and sent to Germany. Clothes, glasses, shoes and blankets were burnt. Often kanada kommandos smuggled some of the valuables and used them later as bribes for the guards.

They also took new shoes and clothes to protect themselves from the winter cold. If caught, the sentence was death. The maximum life expectancy of the in-camp workers was between a week and 4 months. They were considered the elite among the prisoners. The minimum working hours were 11 a day, with one free day a week, usually Sunday.

However, prisoners were given duties around the camp that day too. Cleaning and disinfecting were obligatory, and their free time was used to clean their uniforms from mites, bugs, weed and dirt. Execution by labor was a profitable method of extermination of thousands of Jews. Workers were not only exhausted, hungry and sick; they were also tortured by the guards in the cruelest of ways.

Given that they had to work at least 12 hours a day, it was no surprise that the prisoners either fell sick from exhaustion or just plain dropped dead. In winter, they had to deal with both the backbreaking work as well as the bitter cold that they could not even fight since they were not given any proper clothing.

The number of working hours was supposed to be lesser during the cold months, but suffice to say, the Nazis could hardly be bothered about keeping their inmates healthy. Lumber yard work, gravel pit work and work on construction sites continued on as they ever did, with little no concern for the prisoners' lives.

One would expect that the prisoners would at least be allowed to come back to their camps and relax – one couldn't be more mistaken. Even the use of latrines was monitored; each time they went to the bathroom, they had to not only log it in, but also record the time taken inside the bathroom, which is rather disturbing in and of itself.

The more time they took, the more suspicious the guards became of them, thinking they were up to something inside the latrines.

As I have mentioned, Sunday was supposed to be the prisoners' day off, but even then they had duties assigned to them. While their official work was over, they had to clean and disinfect the barracks and take care of any of the other inmates who had fallen sick. Sunday was also the day when they could take a shower – this was not so much concern on the part of the Nazis for them, as it was just a way to ensure that any sickness did not spread.

Of course, the water they were given was not always hot or even clean, but to the prisoners who spent the entire week slogging it out and being dirty, it ended up being quite the heavenly experience.

Sunday was also the only day that they were allowed to write to their families. As you can probably guess, the SS were not going to let them have free reign here either – the letters they wrote were intercepted by them and carefully scrutinized for any communication beyond the permitted.

This meant that the letters had to be written in German or the prisoners would not only have their letters torn up, but also dragged in for questioning, which, as you can guess, is a euphemistic way of saying that they would be further tortured.

Many a survivor has told stories of how they had to ask their fellow inmates to help write their letters since they did not know German. In exchange for it, they would trade a part of their bread with the person helping out – which, given that they were already being given rationed portions to eat, ended up being detrimental to their health.

And that is not even taking into account the prisoners' scuffles to gain favor with the Nazis; can you imagine how many inmates got into trouble because of their lack of German knowledge and another prisoner's need to gain favor with the SS (therefore writing something incriminating within the letters)?

The weekday was no less painful for them; after they returned from work, being pushed to work for more than ten hours a day, they were still not allowed to rest. They were often made to stand for a second Roll Call in the evening – the morning's Roll Call was bad enough, but can you imagine how much worse it must have been in the evening, about to fall to the ground from exhaustion?

If someone went missing, then the entire camp would be

forced to stand in line until they were found, which sometimes could take hours. Many of the inmates succumbed to death from the combination of the evening's cold and exhaustion.

When finally the Roll Call ended, the guards would then call out the punishments, based on whatever perceived error they had committed that day. Obviously, many of these were something as simple as daring to look up at the guards' eyes or being unable to work from exhaustion or sickness, but the SS cared little for their pain and gleefully punished perceived transgressions.

## Conditions in the Camps

The living conditions in the death camps were inhumane at best. The prisoners were divided in quarters or blocks. Political prisoners were kept separately from the Jews, the homosexuals, Catholic clergies and Jehovah witnesses. The barracks were always overcrowded, damp, leaky and invaded by rats, vermin and other wildlife.

It was only after the punishments were handed out that the prisoners were given their food – this was also allotted in rations. The little bread and water they were given were hardly enough to sustain them and many a scuffle broke out between hungry inmates in their attempts to steal from their neighbors to fill their bellies.

Finally, they were sent to the barracks to sleep. It goes without saying that these were not exactly the most comfortable of places to sleep – they was very little space for each of them. A number of survivors have spoken about how tiny the barracks actually were; thousands of inmates were thrown in together in one room and they were made to lie down, regardless of the fact that they had to be squished and literally molded to one another.

After a long, tiring day of manual labor, they couldn't even stretch out their exhausted limbs, crammed together as they were. And depending on how long the evening Roll Call went, the number of hours they had to rest were limited, especially since the guards refused to delay the early morning Roll Call.

Most of the time, the inmates could not sleep for more than three to four hours, which obviously left them drained and exhausted and unable to work, and therefore, victim to more punishment from the guards. It was a ruthless cycle that killed many.

Dinner, as we saw, was stale bread and water. Breakfast was no better – they were given nowhere near enough food to keep them going through the day for their work. The smallest of portions were meted out, if they were given food at all; many times, the only thing they would get in the mornings was a hot drink before they were put to work.

Lunch was generally vegetable soup, thin and with little broth, leaving them even more hungry and tired. Only those prisoners who had been chosen to serve as guinea pigs for the medical experiments were given proper rations of food and water. But their fates were far, far worse – they were treated as dolls to be played with and put through horrific medical procedures that left many of them scarred and maimed, if they were alive at all.

The camp, as you can guess, was definitely not sanitary. The Nazis could not be bothered to clean up and since the prisoners had only Sunday to clean their spaces, it was really not all that fresh. The lack of hygiene, the lack of space and the close quarters meant that diseases and epidemics spread like wildfire. Inmates dropped like flies and few survived the horrors of Auschwitz.

In Auschwitz II, the barracks were built to house 40 prisoners. However, most of the time there were around 600 people living in the same barrack. Three bunk beds were located in 60 spaces; a layer of straw was used instead of mattresses. The wooden barracks were even worse.

The bottom and the top of the walls had wide gaps, from where wind and rain poured in and soaked the earth floor and beds. Near the entrance, the rooms of the kapos and sondercommandos were located. The conditions there were no different than the barracks, they were just separated.

Toilet facilities consisted of wooden barracks, where two long concrete boards with 100 holes were used as a toilet. All prisoners had to use them before the officers did their Roll Calls. 2000 prisoners had to fight over 100 holes at once. They were given watery soup and one piece of black bread, once in the morning before they went to work, again at noon and in the evening, after work hours.

Some days, some type of sausage was served. Those prisoners who worked usually got back too late, so their soup was either missing or frozen. They had to break the ice and lick it frozen. They were also given some sort of diluted coffee and tea, which they used to wash their hands and face.

Showering time was once a week - Sunday. There was no clean water; they all used the same dirty water. Officers often messed around with the prisoners, telling a few to get ready for showering, when in reality, they would take them in the chambers and "shower" them with gas.

The sanitary conditions of the camps varied by section. Outbreaks of diseases happened all the time. Dysentery, typhus and cholera were the most vicious killers. A pesticide, Zyklon B, was used to disinfect the clothes of the diseased, but later it was used as a poison in gas chambers.

There was a "hospital" behind the walls of the camp. Skilled workers who were too valuable to be gassed, but too sick to work were taken there. There was no medical care and no medications. Amputations were done without anesthesia, until the patients died.

## Punishments

The Nazis main plan was to starve the prisoners to death. Their diets were very poor in nutrients and calories. Every grown man was given up to 1700 calories a day, usually even less. Eventually they developed a state the SS men called Muselmann, which is a combination of starvation and exhaustion that ends in death.

During working hours, the prisoners were supervised by guards. If the guard needed a free day, they would take the prisoner's hat and throw it. They ordered them to fetch it and they would shoot them in the back. When their superiors came, they told them they caught a prisoner trying to escape. This would secure them 3 free days.

Another form of punishment was called flogging. This punishment was carried out during roll calls, on a bench designed so that the person couldn't move their legs. Then, the officers beat the prisoner with a stick, or more commonly a whip.

They were allowed only 25 beatings at once, to avoid killing the prisoners this way. This was a favorite way of punishment for women and children, as it was intimidation with trained dogs.

The pillar was also frequently used for rebelling prisoners. Their hands were tied behind their back and they were hanged by their wrists. Prolonged punishment on the pillar often resulted in agonizing pain, dislocation of shoulders and torn tendons, after which the prisoner would faint.

## Block 10 and 11

The inmates who were taken to have committed transgressions against the Nazis were generally sent to the standing cells – if they were not beaten or tortured to death first. The horror cells were named aptly; the space was so tiny that a single person found it difficult to stand up properly. It was into this miniscule space that they were all thrown in – imagine three or four people trying to squeeze into the space that even one person finds it difficult to fully occupy!

To make matters worse, the prisoners in the standing cells were obviously given no food or water and they were sent there only after they had been beaten up as part of their punishment. Without rations or medicinal aid to recover from their injuries, many of them died right there.

And then there were the dark cells, which were situated in the camp's basement area. With a solid door and the tiniest of windows, the dark cell was every inch the horror prisoner cell – it was a suffocating, dingy dungeon where prisoners were sent to die. In fact, the amount of breathing space in the dark cells was so small, the actual oxygen content cut off so much, that prisoners generally lasted only for a few hours before they suffocated to death.

To make their already painful end come faster, the SS guards who had thrown them in would not think twice about lighting a candle. As you can guess, this was one of the worst psychological tortures inflicted upon the inmates – the candle gave them the light in the dark, but it also ate up what little oxygen they had, quickening their approaching death.

The standing cells and dark cells were a dreadful, but very popular punishment in most camps during the Reich. The cells in the main camp were 1.5 square meters, and up to 5 people were stuffed in there as penalty if they overstepped their boundaries and asked for another bowl of the watery soup.

The cell had only one small window or opening, which was covered with a metal lid. Prisoners were punished with standing there from one night, to 20 nights in a row. During the day, they still had to work. Sometimes, the guards would light up a candle to soak up the oxygen and force the prisoners to suffocate. Starvation cells were also located here, where prisoners were locked without food or water until they died.

One famous sadist among the SS unit was Wilhelm Boger, who invented a swing (Boger Swing) designed for torturing. The swing had two crossed stalks at each side, holding a metal pole on their top. This metal pole was placed behind the prisoners knees, while their hands were tied to their ankles on their feet.

The pole was then raised by the guards and placed on top of the stalks, from where the prisoners hung with their heads down. They were swung while questioning, beaten with sticks and whips, until they fainted. Then they were woken up and beaten again.

Most prisoners didn't survive this torture, and the floor was black from blood, and bodies were carried out of this basement after every interrogation. Boger was one of the most merciless officers in the Reich. One of the guards who testified later in the Auschwitz Trial said he saw him beating a naked woman so severely, that he tore her breast off and flooded the room with blood.

While the basement cells of block 10 were used for torture, the basement of block 11 was designed for medical experiments. Bruno Weber, Eduard Wirths and August Hirt were several doctors in charge of the experiments. Carl Clauberg and Horst Schumann were two doctors whose experiments focused around sterilization.

The space between block 10 and 11 was used for executing prisoners by shooting. The blocks were connected with walls on both sides; one of the walls was called the Wall Of Death. The center of the wall was of wooden construction to prevent the bullets from bouncing back and the ground was covered with sand, to soak up the victim's blood.

They were usually shot in pairs, although group shootings

were executed too. Prisoners were stripped naked and forced to wait outside for the shooters. Around 20,000 people were killed by shooting against this wall.

# Chapter 5: Angels of Death and the Crematoria

Sometimes, it is considered that death is a gift. That is true in the case of the Jews who were brought into Auschwitz. Death could have been a merciful act as compared to the other horrors the camp held for them. More than the strenuous labor and the mass killings, it was the medical experiments that are capable of curdling the reader's blood.

Walking to the gas chamber would seem like a simpler and easier way to end their fates than subject them to medical experiments. In this chapter, we bring to you the gruesome details of the human experimentation that was being carried on at Auschwitz.

**Medical experiments:**

The German doctors who were residing at the camp were known to have conducted a lot of medical experiments on the prisoners of the camp. These experiments varied in terms of the degree of cruelty associated with them. The female prisoners were subject to large doses of X-rays to test if the X-rays were capable of exhibiting sterilization properties.

Chemicals were injected into the wombs of the female prisoners in an attempt to check if these chemicals were capable of gluing their uteruses shut. Most prisoners were subject to experiments that involved them getting infected with spotted fever. This was done so to develop vaccinations and a cure for spotted fever.

Children were not spared from these horrific experiments either. Around twenty Jewish children were made the subjects of certain medical experiments that were pseudo-scientific in nature. However, these children were later hanged to death to conceal the damages of these unconventional experiments.

## Angel of Death and other Prison Guards

Dr. Josef Mengele was dubbed as the Angel of Death because of the notoriety associated with his experiments. He was known to have had a specific interest in choosing twins for his experiments. He would administer one twin with disease inducing virus and wait for the person to die. Once the victim died, the other twin would be killed by the Doctor. He would then conduct an autopsy on both their corpses to gauge the damage of the disease.

Ideally, he used the twins to conduct a comparative study on the human anatomy by doing autopsies on them at the same time. He was also interested in experimenting with dwarves. He was known to have induced Noma in many twins. Noma is a bacterial infection that usually cropped up among the people who were malnourished.

The Angel of Death also did not operate by himself. He had a number of companions who assisted him in his horrendous work; of these, perhaps the most infamous was the woman who came to be known later as the Hyena of Auschwitz.

Irma Grese was a notorious female SS guard whose cruelty and brutality to the inmates of the camp knew no bounds. Not for nothing was she known as a Hyena – she loved to whip the prisoners under her care, set her ferocious dogs on them and often left them lying in the cold, maimed and hurt.

Rumor had it that she and Mengele were lovers. Later confirmed, the two of them slaughtered hundreds of prisoners without a shred of mercy – they were quite the dynamic duo, a dark Harlequin Romance that destroyed more innocent lives than we can count.

Let me tell you about Dr. Mengele first. That his nickname was 'The Angel of Death' by itself should be telling – he was the doctor in charge of leading all the experiments on the prisoners and he took great pleasure in concocting new and bizarre procedures that killed hundreds.

He joined the Nazis in the year 1937, initially taking up the position of a soldier in the German Armed Forces. But that didn't appeal to him all that much and it wasn't long before he signed up to serve in the medical service of the combat section of the SS.

It was in the year 1942 that he was wounded in action and sent back home, unfit for battle. But he did not want to stop being a part of the Nazis and decided to find another way to contribute to their brutality; he applied for a transfer to the concentration camps. Rumors were flying around at the time that Hitler was ordering medical experiments be conducted upon the inmates in the camps and as a doctor, the thought of performing uncontrolled procedures excited him.

It didn't take long before he was given the position of chief physician at Auschwitz – he had both medical training and a doctorate in anthropology from the University of Munich to back him up.

It was around this time that the sub-camp at Birkenau was repurposed – from the labor camp it had been, it was now turned into an extermination camp. The unfortunate victims in these camps were all those that the Nazis deemed unworthy of life, since they could not perform the back breaking labor to 'contribute' to German Society.

The inmates ranged from the elderly and the sick to pregnant women and children and nursing mothers who could not perform the harsh physical labor.

Mengele was put in charge of the selection of the inmates who would be sent to the extermination camp, to their deaths. He didn't send them there right away; he wanted to find subjects for his experiments and observed them like lab rats, treating them as his own personal play things.

What is disturbing is that he seemed to have enjoyed both his experiments as well as the selection process itself – many survivors report that he would often hum, whistle and smile as he sent the inmates to the death row, fully believing in Hitler's ideology of racial superiority.

He headed the team of prison doctors who were meant to care for sick prisoners within the camps. Obviously, he didn't exactly give them the rosy treatment; as he made his rounds, if he discovered that any inmate was in the sick bay for more than two weeks or so, he sent them to be gassed without the slightest hesitation.

In his mind, they were not working and were not worth the resources it would take to nurse them back to health and hence, had to be exterminated like insects. He was also part of the team of SS doctors who would administer the pesticide Zyklon B in the gas chambers to kill the inmates.

As we have seen, epidemic outbreak in the concentration camps was a common occurrence and as I already mentioned, Noma was one major disease that spread very quickly. A disease of bacterial origin, it is gangrenous in nature, which means that it can pose threat to life and limbs if not treated properly.

Mengele undertook the study to identify what the cause of the disease was and how to stop it. It sounds nice when put like that, but in reality, what Mengele did was nothing but the execution of cold, calculated cruelty.

Every single inmate who had been infected by the disease was sent to a separate barrack, segregated from the general fold. Out of them, the Angel of Death picked out a handful of children and had them taken out separately – he had them murdered one by one and then cut up their bodies to remove their heads as well as other organs. These were then carefully packaged and sent to the Medical Army's facilities for further research.

His sadism did not stop there, rearing its ugly head once more when then typhus epidemic overtook the barracks in the women's camps. Mengele was meant to disinfect the camp and he did it – literally. He cleared one of the blocks fully, sending the six hundred or so women imprisoned there to their deaths by having them gassed; it was to stop the spread of the infection, he cited.

The women in the neighbouring block – as of yet unaffected by the epidemic – were then called out into the open, where they were made to strip, hosed down and bathed. They were given new clothes before they were sent to stay in another block that was cleaner and did not reek of infection.

This treatment was meted out again and again – all the inmates in infected blocks were simply killed and the neighbouring blocks were disinfected and then relocated. In literal terms, Mengele treated them like they were his own personal cattle stock and didn't care the slightest bit that they were real people who had real lives.

The brutality of his actions are not to be questioned, but since he managed to put a stop to the spread of the epidemic, the Nazis awarded him with the War Merit Cross instead of being horrified at his actions. That the thousands of innocents who were killed might have survived under proper care and medication didn't matter in the least – he stopped the epidemic and therefore deserved an award.

And then there were the human experiments. As I said before, the main reason he wanted to be stationed at the Auschwitz camp as part of the medical team was because he was given free reign of human test subjects.

The Nazis could care less about their safety or their lives – at least, were they sacrificed in the pursuit of science, their lives would mean something because they had, in some way, contributed to the Third Reich. It was this mentality that prevailed amongst the guards and Mengele lived with this ideology to the extent that he treated the inmates as his own expendable lab rats, using them and then disposing of them as he saw fit.

He was particularly interested in the idea of identical twins. He also harboured a special interest people with 'heterochromia iridum', a condition where the victims are blessed with two different eye colours. Apart from that, he showed interest in anyone with a physical abnormality, having them sent to his labs to perform horrific experiments on them.

The news of his experiments spread so fast and gained so much fame that he was ordered to have a pathology lab built at Auschwitz II-Birkenau. He was given a government grant to further continue his research and Hitler even had special 'shipments' of 'specimens' sent to him.

One survivor, a man by the name of Dr. Miklós Nyiszli, was forced to work under Mengele at the camp. He himself was a Jewish doctor from Hungary who had been deported to Auschwitz with his wife and his daughter. Once they got to the camp, he went to volunteer at the medical station, given how poor the conditions were and how many of the inmates were sick.

But there, instead of caring for the ill, he was made to perform sick experiments on them. Some of the horror stories he recalls are extremely disturbing – Mengele would have him dissect living people, without giving them any sort of anaesthesia to reduce the pain, have him prepare the 'specimen' for further study, perform autopsies on those who were murdered, and more such horrific procedures.

Nyiszli reports – corroborated by many of the other Auschwitz survivors – that Mengele wanted to find out why the Jewish race were so inferior to them. He firmly believed that the idea had a scientific basis instead of moralistic or idealistic origin and turned to medical experimentation to figure out the cause of their 'inferiority' and then attempt to wipe it out completely. To that extent, he didn't care about how many people he killed or maimed; in the grand picture, they were irrelevant and didn't matter in the least.

Mengele also used Darwin's theories on Natural Selection and Survival of the Fittest as basis for his experiments; his research on twins was carried out with the purpose of proving that the hereditary genes were higher when it came to the hierarchy of the natural environment.

He also was fascinated with twins because they granted him the opportunity to improve the rate of reproduction within the country. If those who were 'racially desirable' could produce twins instead of just one child, then Germany's entire population would soon be reconfigured to have only the sections that Hitler wanted.

As we already saw, the living conditions within the barracks were pathetic and horrendous; millions died from lack of proper care and simple hygiene. Those who were selected to be part of Mengele's experiments were treated extra well. They were given proper food and water rations, allowed them good hygiene and kept them in the best of health. They were treated as special because they were chosen to be the sacrificial lambs of his experiments.

What is even more chilling is Mengele's attitude towards the children. Unlike what you might expect, the man did not act hostile with them in the least – in fact, he treated them like a long lost uncle, giving them treats and gifts and playing with them.

He went so far as to have a kindergarten constructed within campgrounds – meant only for the children he had handpicked to be his lab rats. Until such a time when they would be called to be studied and experimented upon, they lived in this block, which had better living conditions than the entire camp. There was good food, fresh running water and even a playground for the kids to play in.

His interactions with the kids will give even the strongest people nightmares – he introduced himself to the unknowing victims as 'Uncle Mengele', played with them and often gave them sweets. Children, as you can guess, are innocent and guileless.

They were terrified of him, but they followed him around and fell in love with the things he offered them. They had very little in the way of affection or love, and his token items made them happy – a fact he used to the maximum advantage.

Mengele was the worst kind of monster – he was kind to them until his kindness turned to cruelty. He would, at first, offer them sweets and candy and fix their problems, which were not little in number, given that they lived in concentration camps. He earned their trust, became their friend and companion and then, he turned right around and had them packed off to the labs, where they were cut up, tortured and then died horrible deaths.

Twins were sent in every week to be examined for their physical characteristics, after which, the doctors were to perform bizarre procedures on them in an attempt to identify and duplicate their racial superiority/inferiority.

The horrors these children faced are spine chilling – they had their limbs cut off and amputated, one twin would be infected on purpose with a deadly disease like typhus after which the other twin's blood would be transfused into his body to observe its reaction, both twins were murdered at one go so that their autopsies could be conducted simultaneously, etc.

Nyiszli recounted one night when Mengele personally killed fourteen twins at one go. He injected their little hearts with chloroform and then had their bodies autopsied for various things. If one twin died before the other, then the remaining twin's life was automatically doomed. Mengele decreed that their deaths happen so that simultaneous post mortems could be performed and the reports compared.

Another witness reported how he had two twins, of Romani origin, sewn together. He was trying to create conjoined twins by doing so; it goes without saying that the kids did not survive this. Their deaths weren't even kind or painless – Mengele watched in fascination as gangrene set in, instead of them becoming conjoined, and within a few days, they both passed away. They were both in a considerable amount of pain, not that the Angel of Death cared one bit.

The experiments that Mengele conducted upon adults were no less spine chilling. Those with heterochromatic eyes were specially brought to camp because he requested such 'specimens' from the Third Reich.

These people, upon arrival in the camp, were whisked away to be experimented upon – they had their eyes removed and the samples were sent to Berlin for further study. As we know, Hitler believed that fair haired and blue eyed people of the Aryan race were the most racially superior and desirable – Mengele wanted to change people's eye colours to bring out that expected colour. To do that, he injected a number of victims with a variety of chemicals – few survived, and of those, almost all lost their eyesight or suffered other side effects.

Author of 'The Fifth Diamond', Irene Zisblatt, recounted her time under Mengele's thumb. She confirmed that Mengele was attempting to change the eye colours of people and spoke of the horrors these victims faced. They were injected with a variety of strange chemical combinations, following which they were sent to be kept in a dark, dungeon like space, which was damp and cramped.

Few of these victims survived and 3 out of 5 of them lost their eyesight. Zisblatt herself managed to get out of there, but her eyes remained green as they always were – obviously, Mengele's madness had absolutely no effect on his victims.

People with other physical abnormalities were treated abominably. Dwarfs' blood was drawn repeatedly and their physical measurements were taken without their permission, following which their teeth were pulled out without any anaesthesia. They were sent for X-Ray enough times that many died from too much radiation exposure, and a number of them were injected with random, experimental drugs that really didn't have a purpose.

Mengele's experiments on one group of people rarely exceeded a week; like a child with a new toy, he tired of them very quickly and kept sending for 'newer specimens'. Once he was bored of them, he had no use for them – he sent them to the gas chambers were they were killed without hesitation. The dead skeletons were then packed off to Berlin for further research.

Almost all doctors of the Reich exercised medicine on the prisoners. Schumann took people of good health, teenage prisoners and those in their 20's. He used X-Rays to sterilize them. Women were pressed with two plates, at their back and stomach. Men's genitals and scrotum was placed on a specially designed plate.

Intestinal damage, radiation burns and cancer usually killed these patients, if they didn't make it to the gas chamber. His colleague, Clauberg sterilized his victims with injections. He sterilized only women of proven fertility, by injecting different substances directly into their cervix.

Freezing and hypothermia experiments involved freezing the victims in icy pits or being naked outside in the cold. Two Russian prisoners were the only ones who didn't faint after a short amount of time, but the temperature was lowered until they died. Warming experiments were not pleasant either.

One homosexual was cooled until he fainted, then warmed up under a sun lamp, for several sessions, until he too, died. Some prisoners were warmed up in hot baths, where the water temperature slowly increased.

They died of shock. Himmler suggested that the men were warmed up by women prisoners, who would copulate with them to increase their temperature.

New drugs and medications were tested on already diseased prisoners. The true names of the drugs were rarely used, records showed people injected with medications marked B-1012, 3582, B-1034, P-111, B-1036, and similar. Pregnant mothers were always taken for experiments. Mengele took the newborn and left it in cold/heat, unfed and cared for, to see how long they would survive.

Gas chambers and crematoria were in both Auschwitz I and II. The ones in the main camp were out of order once the bigger camp was built, 50 kilometers away. The gas chambers were underground, with openings at the top, from where the SS men poured the gas.

From there, the bodies were transferred into the crematoria, which were either nearby or right next to the gas chamber. Some of the records confiscated from the Nazis show that between 300 to 2000 bodies were burnt every day in the crematoria.

Most of them are demolished today, you can only visit one. The walls are still tainted blue from the gas and there are scratches from nails on the walls.

# Irma Grese

As we have already seen, Joseph Mengele was not alone in his torture. Accompanying him was his lover, Irma Grese, the Hyena of Auschwitz. She was a nasty piece of work indeed; beautiful and sadistic, she took immense pleasure in causing harm to the prisoners under her care and didn't care the slightest bit about their welfare.

While this has not really been confirmed, a number of sources say that she was trained by none other than Theodora Binz herself. For those unaware, Binz was yet another female guard who had no qualms about whipping and maiming the prisoners under her care.

Grese's own whipping technique and skills came from her mentor – Binz was known to crack her whip at unsuspecting victims whenever she perceived a transgression, which was a practice her protégée, Grese, would later adopt happily. Binz was also a sadist and enjoyed causing pain – there are stories about how she once hacked a woman inmate to bits using an axe because she felt that the woman wasn't working as hard as she should be.

Evidently, once she was done murdering the woman and mutilating her corpse, she simply wiped the blood off her boots and then jumped back on to her bike, which she rode to camp as she happily whistled under her breath.

If Grese truly did train under a woman such as that, it comes as no surprise that she turned out to be so sadistic and cruel. Interestingly, the Nazis, being the epitome of sexist and hate, had strict policies about training guards, especially the female ones. A large number of them – male and female – quit when they were forced to undergo these training regimens.

During these, they were made to handpick prisoners who were lined up for them and then beat them mercilessly, without showing the slightest hint of sympathy. Man or woman, this kind of brutality is hard to perform, but the Nazis felt that the female species had 'delicate' sensibilities that would prove an extra hindrance. Grese proved them all wrong – she enjoyed this process and excelled at it. She passed with flying colors, especially since she invented new games to play with the inmates, such as having them turn on one another simply to win her favor.

Nine months of such sadistic training and Grese joined Mengele at the Auschwitz camp, where she quickly rose within the ranks. In May of 1944, she was given control of over thirty thousand female inmates in her stead as the Oberaufseherin, and she took to power like duck to water, abusing it in every which way possible.

Along with Mengele and another female guard called Margot Elisabeth Dreschler (equally sadistic and cruel), Grese was put in charge of the selection process. As is obvious, the process of picking who would be gassed to death had no exact science behind it; generally, who ever made Grese and her companions angry were sent to the chambers to be killed off.

Grese also had the job of finding those who tried to escape their fate. A number of prisoners tried to hide out within the camps to save their lives from the gas chambers and Grese not only ferreted them out, but made an example out of them by beating and torturing them to death in front of the other inmates, amongst whom the victims' family members were also usually present.

Once, Mengele and Grese personally sent over three thousand victims to the gas chambers to be killed. When victims tried to escape by hiding themselves under the beds, Grese went to personally hunt them down and then cracked her whip, beating them senseless until they fell unconscious, if they survived. Those who did survive her beatings, she dragged to the gas chambers herself, where they were put to death instantly.

Grese was, apparently, even more cruel than Mengele.

There was one instance when Mengele had had a woman cleared for labor. The inmate was a prisoner who had been deported to the Auschwitz camp from a ghetto in Iza. Mengele believed that she was fit and good enough to work within the camp; Grese protested, saying that she didn't *"...like the way she walked..."* and was all set to send her to the gas chambers for that perceived transgression.

Survivors recall that Grese looked every inch the Blonde Bitch of Auschwitz as she was called. Grese was physically quite beautiful; she cut a striking figure, especially since she took to accentuating her natural features into something fierce with her clothing and accessories.

Her suit was tailored to fit her in all the right places and she wore powerful boots that gave her the illusion of strength and height. When it came to weaponry, she carried around her trusty whip and a pistol, even though Nazi regulations forbade female guards from carrying arms.

But the most terrifying weapon she had were her ferocious dogs. The animals were almost feral and she kept them in a state of constant hunger, underfeeding them on purpose – when an inmate crossed a line, she was known to beat them and then set her dogs on them to finish her job. Given their feral nature, it didn't take long for them to rip the poor victim apart, gorging themselves on their flesh.

Grese's whip was synonymous with her name; she never went anywhere without it and took sadistic pleasure in beating up her inmates with it. Not only was it long and made of cellophane to make the lacerations deeper, she also had a braided wire attached to the end to cause as much pain as she could to better 'control' her unruly prisoners. If she wasn't whipping the women under her care, she was beating them to death with the stick/club she carried.

As I said before, if an inmate did survive her beatings, Grese would set their dogs on them, who would then tear them apart. A number of these victims would attempt to escape by trying to run to the borders of the camp; given their injuries and their exhaustion due to overworking and malnourishment, they died horrible deaths – the dogs, already feral and wild, were thrilled at the idea of a chase and literally pounced on these victims and tore them to bits.

One survivor recalls how Grese would set the dogs on those who could not perform the work given to them. Malnourished and overworked and exhausted as they were, the inmates would often be unable to finish the workload, which was expected to be completed in unrealistic timelines. The survivor told a story of how they had all been working hard and how they kept their heads low as to avoid Grese's attention.

The team behind them, however, were unfortunate – they were so nervous that they lost control of the wagon, which they had to push up the hill. The wagon rolled down, taking with it all the rocks they were to transport to the other side – it capsized and the rocks scattered around the area, causing a mess.

Grese had simply sent her dogs out on the entire team. The women, desperate to survive, ran helter skelter to protect themselves, but they were outmatched by the ferocity of the dogs. The first to die was a Polish inmate, who unfortunately, tripped on a rock and fell down – the dogs pounced on her and tore her to bits.

The next to go was a Russian woman and then one by one, almost all of them were victim to the dogs. Those who did survive the attack, Grese beat up mercilessly along with the other guards by her side – their bodies lay on the hillside for the dogs to gorge on, not even treated with the basic human dignity they deserved.

The most disturbing thing, perhaps, about Grese, is that she was *sexually* aroused by all the cruelty she caused. More than one survivor has testified to the truth of this –

Grese found sexual fulfilment in causing pain and suffering to those around her.

A survivor, who had been deported to Auschwitz from Budapest, stated that Grese would march into camp and randomly beat up the inmates with her club and moan erotically at the sight of them writhing in pain. This would happen most often in the bath barracks – naked or otherwise, the women would try to escape and in the pandemonium, a number of them were trampled and suffocated to death, at which point Grese would often hit her climax.

She invented new and sadistic games for the inmates to play in – did they not follow her conditions and rules, they were beat up and killed. Daily beatings were to be expected and torture was a part of the inmates' lives.

Grese would punish them for the lightest perceived transgression such as not standing straight during roll call. She would have them hold up heavy rocks above their heads – the inmates were to stand for hours continuously with this kind of torture. If they dropped their hands or tried to get some kind of relief, they would be beaten to death – the moment they fell to the ground, Grese would kick them until they bled.

Grese was particularly irritated with women who were

considered to be traditionally beautiful and/or well endowed with plenty of curves. She would have them strip publicly, humiliate them and then whip them across their breasts, for no reason other than that they were beautiful.

A number of the survivors, including famous Jewish obstetrician Dr. Gisella Pearl, testified to the obsession Grese had with maiming women's breasts. More often than not, these women would catch infection from the unhygienic conditions they were exposed to. If they tried to receive medical help, Mengele and his passé would pounce on them to be used as lab rats; they died from the surgeries they were made to undergo, usually without anaesthesia.

Dr. Pearl has described in detail how much Grese enjoyed torturing her victims and how she found sexual release in it. She talks of how the Beautiful Beast of Auschwitz would come to the hospital barracks, where Pearl would treat those with infected breasts. The doctor was given no anaesthesia to help them get through the surgeries; Grese would watch with hooded eyes as these women screamed from the pain. She would then go on to pleasure herself as their cries of pain grew louder and louder.

Grese also sexually abused a number of her inmates. The maiming of the breasts was just the tip of the iceberg; it goes without saying that at a concentration camp, the victims were helpless to the guards' advances. Grese was one of these guards who made passes at a number of the prisoners, who had little choice but to accept her passes.

If they didn't, they would be tortured to death – if they did, they would be living in fear of constant threat, since sexuality was a big question mark in those days and Grese's love of women as a woman herself would have had her ostracized, which meant that she needed her victims to keep quiet about her activities. She went about threatening them to keep their mouths shut, and in fear of her, they did.

The true nature of the perversion of Grese's mind came to fore at her trial, after Auschwitz had been liberated by the Allies. She plead as *not guilty* to all the charges – she truly believed that she had committed no wrong. There was a witness who testified to a story where Grese killed a daughter for simply speaking to her mother across the compound, through a barbed wire.

Grese rode up on her bike, threw the mother away from the wire and then proceeded to beat her senseless with her whip, following which she kicked and stamped her until she was almost dead. The victim spent the next three weeks at the hospital barracks and never fully recovered.

When this story was narrated on the stand, Grese

responded with a callousness that is telling of the disturbed mind she possessed –

*"I do not deny that I beat her, but I did not beat her until she fell to the ground, and I did*

*not kick her either."*

Her response is truly disturbing, as though she didn't care one whit about any human life.

And this was the truth about life at the Auschwitz concentration camp – be it Mengele, Grese or any of the other SS guards, few were given to care of the prisoners under their command.

They took sadistic pleasure in harming these unsuspecting victims and whipped, beat, raped and tortured them until each day became hell on earth for the inmates. Physical, sexual, emotional and psychological abuse was heaped on them without hesitation and it's no wonder that so few of them survived.

# Chapter 6: The Fall of the Nazis and the Jewish Liberation

There were several escape attempts from many death camps during Nazi Germany. Some of them were successful, but most ended tragically. The punishment was public hanging. There were several stationary hanging gallows and many mobile ones.

In October 1943, one woman snatched the pistol from an officer who waited for several women to undress and enter the gas chamber. Other women tried to do the same, but eventually they were seized and killed on the spot. They managed to kill one SS officer.

One night in May 1944, several men, women and children were found hiding in the ditches and woods. They were killed on the spot.

Very few escaped from Auschwitz. In several organized attempts, prisoners stole uniforms, ID's and even a vehicle from the SS guards. They managed to escape the wired walls, by yelling at the guards at the main gate, pretending to be SS officers. Most of them were found days later. After these well thought-out attempts, the guards gassed 300 Poles as a sign of revenge and to prevent other resistance.

# The Liberation

It remains controversial as to why the Allies did not do more during the holocaust. In the beginning, the Nazis sent prisoners to death camps while telling the world that they were only relocating them in the east. Later, the great powers had access to documentation of everything that was happening in many death camps, except for Auschwitz.

For many years, Jewish prisoners were occasionally allowed to write letters to their relatives as long as they didn't mention the massacres. In 1943, prisoner Malka Zimetbaum alertly wrote to her sister: "Don't worry. I am in good health. I'm working as an interpreter."

Many governments were notified with warnings. None of them investigated behind the relocation of the Jews from Germany. Neutral countries like Sweden, Switzerland, Portugal or Turkey didn't offer a safe haven for the refugees.

Finally, American, Canadian, British and French forces started to occupy German controlled grounds on 6th of June, 1944. Weeks later, Soviet forces started their offensive and by August 1944, they took control all the way through Central Poland. When the Germans realized they were losing ground, they demolished the camps to destroy the evidence of the holocaust and ordered most of the prisoners to march west to Germany.

This was known as the March of Death, since thousands of people perished in the cold or from starvation. Many were shot on their way to freedom. When the Soviet forces liberated Auschwitz in January 1945, there were only 7,650 prisoners, most of them children. Many people didn't survive even after the liberation.

They were sick for months from malaria, tuberculosis and other terminal diseases. Hitler committed suicide on April 30th, the Nazis surrendered on the 8th of May 1945. Only an estimated 15% of the Nazis responsible for the holocaust were sentenced. Many were acquitted, most returned to the jobs they had before the war. Suicides with cyanide pills were not uncommon, which was a Nazi way of preserving the "pride and dignity" of the Aryan race.

## Post War

Auschwitz, post the war, went through strange transformations. The main camp, Auschwitz I was converted into a hospital of all things – those who were liberated were, in fact, sent back to the same place where they were torture, this time to recuperate with proper care and medical aid. In a strange and fitting way, it was closure and many survivors were able to get proper treatment for all their injuries in the same place where they had been maimed in the first place.

In the mean time, the Soviet and the Polish liberators were investigating the war crimes and trying to find evidence to convict all the SS guards and Nazi soldiers who had committed atrocities during the war. Many a raid was conducted at the Auschwitz camp to find documentation and any other evidence that could put away the SS soldiers and close to eight hundred of those who served as staff at the camp were brought to trial as war criminals.

Trials were held over the course of the next few months, wherein a number of the staff, including the doctors and guards were convicted and then sentenced.

Given that the Auschwitz camp served as both an industrial facility as well as an extermination centre, it is given a special page in the bloody history that is the Holocaust. It was liberated on the 27th of January, a day that is recognized even now as the International Holocaust Remembrance Day, declared as such by the UN General Assembly.

Today, there exists in its place the Auschwitz-Birkenau State Museum, which was established in the year 1947.

The Polish government wanted to erect a state memorial in honor of all the victims who had been subject to the Nazi cruelty during the Holocaust and so; the State Museum came into being.

Later, in the year 1955, the Museum also opened up an exhibition, wherein the remnants from the camps were displayed. Mug shots of the prisoners, canisters containing pellets of Zyklon B that was used in the gas chambers, suitcases and valuables left behind or taken away from the prisoners and other items are on display, showing the world the cruelty that was once widespread, serving as a reminder of just how depraved humanity can really be.

In the year 1979, the Museum was declared as a World Heritage Site by the UNESCO and to this day, it has a huge number of visitors, given its blatant display of Nazi cruelty and the harsh reality that many shy away from.

# Conclusion

Thank you again for purchasing this book!

It is said that if you don't remember history, you are bound to repeat it. Those black and white photos we often see, with starved people who look like skeletons may seem surreal and far from our reality.

The rest of the world was shocked too, when they first saw what was happening to the Jewish people, while they were restfully minding their own business. Don't let those pictures fade in your mind. Let it be a reminder that some day, another Hitler may well be born.

A man who will hypnotize millions of other people into believing that your race or religion is not worth thriving under the sun. Let it be a lesson that will teach us how to recognize the atmosphere of terror and oppression. Just like Anne Frank said: "If we bear all this suffering and if there are still Jews left, when it is over, then Jews, instead of being doomed, will be held up as an example"

If you enjoyed this book, do you think you could leave me a review on Amazon? Just search for this title and my name on Amazon to find it. Thank you so much, it is very much appreciated!

# Want more books?

Would you love books delivered straight to your inbox every week?

Free?

How about non-fiction books on all kinds of subjects?

We send out e-books to our loyal subscribers every week to download and enjoy!

All you have to do is join! It's so easy!

Just visit the link below to sign up and then wait for your books to arrive!

www.LibraryBugs.com

Enjoy :)

Printed in Great Britain
by Amazon

35055691R00051